PICTUREPEDIA

NOTE TO PARENTS

This book is part of PICTUREPEDIA, a completely
new kind of information series for children.
Its unique combination of pictures and words
encourages children to use their eyes to discover and
explore the world, while introducing them to a wealth
of basic knowledge. Clear, straightforward text
explains each picture thoroughly and provides
additional information about the topic.

"Looking it up" becomes an easy task with
PICTUREPEDIA, an ideal first reference for all types of
schoolwork. Because PICTUREPEDIA is also entertaining,
children will enjoy reading its words and looking
at its pictures over and over again. You can encourage
and stimulate further inquiry by helping your child
pose simple questions for the whole family to
"look up" and answer together.

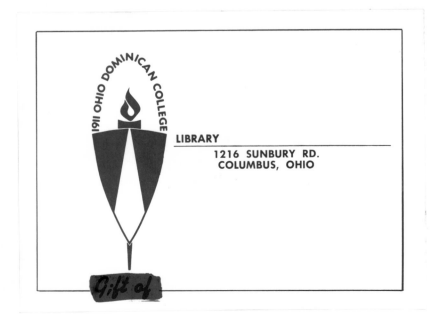

FOOD AND FARMING

A DORLING KINDERSLEY BOOK

Conceived, edited, and designed by DK Direct Limited

Consultant Liza Dibble,
Royal Agricultural College
Project Editor Roz Fishel
Designers Sarah Goodwin,
Wayne Blades, James Hunter
U.S. Editor B. Alison Weir
Series Editor Sarah Phillips
Series Art Editor Paul Wilkinson
Picture Researcher Miriam Sharland
Production Manager Ian Paton
Production Assistant Harriet Maxwell
Editorial Director Jonathan Reed
Design Director Ed Day

First American edition, 1993
4 6 8 10 9 7 5
Published in the United States by
Dorling Kindersley, Inc., 232 Madison Avenue
New York, New York 10016

Library of Congress Cataloging-in-Publication Data
Dibble, Lisa
    Food and farming / Lisa Dibble. — 1st American ed.
    p.   cm. — (Picturepedia)
    Includes index.
    Summary: An illustrated overview of how various foods are
cultivated and used.
    ISBN 1-56458-387-2
    1. Agriculture—Juvenile literature. 2. Food—Juvenile literature
[1. Agriculture. 2. Food.] I. Title. II. Series.
S519.D53   1993
630—dc20   93-19073
                                                        CIP
                                                        AC

Reproduced by Colourscan, Singapore
Printed and bound in Italy by Graphicom

FOOD AND FARMING

DK

DORLING KINDERSLEY

LONDON • NEW YORK
STUTTGART

CONTENTS

WHEAT

What do breakfast cereals, breads, cakes, pastries, pasta, and couscous have in common? The answer is that they are made out of wheat, the most important crop in the world. Wheat is the main food eaten every day by 35 percent of the world's people. It is so important, it is called a staple food. Like barley, oats, rye, corn, rice, sorghum, and millet, wheat is a cereal. Cereals are grasses, and we eat their seeds.

Crop Rotation

If the same crop is grown on the same land year after year, the soil loses its fertility, and pests and diseases build up. The farmer can prevent this by changing the crops grown each year. In the first year, rapeseed may be grown, then wheat, fava beans, wheat again, and barley.

rapeseed

barley

wheat

fava beans

wheat

Machine Power

This is a combine harvester. It cuts the crop and separates the grain from the straw.

This is the unloading spout. It is used to empty threshed grain from the harvester.

In the harvester, the grain is shaken off the stalks. The stalks fall to the ground at the back.

These are straw walkers. They carry the crop through the machine.

Edible Ears

Other cereal crops include oats, barley, and rye. Like wheat, these plants have an "ear" of grain on each stem. Each grain is protected by a husk, and inside the husk is the seed. The grain can be eaten whole or ground into flour.

Rye

Barley

Oats

Wheat Products

Wheat can be used for many different foods. You would never guess that these items are all made from the same ingredient.

Wheat germ

Cracked wheat

Breakfast cereal

Pasta

Monsters on the Move

These wheat fields in the prairies of Manitoba, Canada, are so vast that several combine harvesters can work the fields at the same time.

The cab is air-conditioned to protect the driver from the heat and the dust.

An ear of wheat is made up of 40 to 60 grains. When wheat is ripe and ready for harvesting, it turns golden yellow.

Home Sweet Home

The wheat field is a world of its own. It is home to mammals, insects, birds, and wildflowers.

The reel sweeps the crop into the cutter bar. The cutter bar cuts the crop.

CORN

In many tropical and subtropical countries, corn, or maize, is the main food that people eat. It is eaten as a vegetable or ground into flour or cornmeal. Corn is also made into oil for cooking and for salad dressings. Corn needs lots of sunshine to grow. It will grow in hot climates and also in cooler, mild ones as long as there is plenty of sun. However, the varieties of corn grown in these different climates are not the same.

The flower at the top of the plant is called the tassel.

This is the stalk. Some kinds of corn have stalks as high as 20 feet (6 meters).

Corn is a huge grass.

These long, soft threads are called the silk.

The corn ear, or cob, is protected by a husk of tightly wrapped leaves.

The cob is covered in neat, straight rows of kernels. The kernels are the plant's seeds and the part you eat.

Pest Problems
In warm and tropical areas, one of the pests most feared by farmers is the locust. Locusts travel in huge swarms of over 50 billion insects, stripping plants of their leaves and stems as they feed. Locusts can destroy crops and cause famine and starvation.

Short side roots spread over the surface of the soil. They anchor the tall plant like the guy ropes of a tent and keep it from falling over.

Deep roots go down into the soil and take out the food and water the plant needs to grow.

Sun Ripened

Corn is the staple food of the warmer parts of North, Central, and South America, and also of Africa. It can be grown in huge fields with the help of machinery or on small plots where the crop is tended by hand.

Sweet corn

Breakfast cereal

Mountain of Corn

After the corn has been harvested, it is sorted. Some will be kept as seed for the next crop, some kept for food, and some used as animal feed.

Tortilla chips

Cornucopia of Color

Corn comes in all sorts of colors. It may even be striped, streaked, speckled, or spotted.

Taco

Tough Grains

In dry parts of Africa and Asia, people eat mainly sorghum and millet. These cereals are tough and will grow with little water. This woman is pounding sorghum grain. It is mixed with water or milk until it becomes soft and sticky, like farina. Sorghum is eaten with spicy stews, which give it flavor. It is also ground into flour. Millet is cooked like oatmeal, baked into a flat bread, or used in soups and stews.

Corn oil

RICE

Like corn and wheat, rice is a staple food. It is the main food of over half the world's population – around 2.5 billion people. Ninety percent of the world's rice is grown in Asia. However, the Asian countries eat most of what they grow. The United States also produces huge amounts of rice, but sells much of what it grows to the rest of the world.

Rice is a swamp plant. It grows with its roots in water. It has hollow stems, which take oxygen to the roots.

In Asia, the work of sowing, planting the seedlings, and harvesting the rice is usually done by hand.

How the Rice Plant Is Used

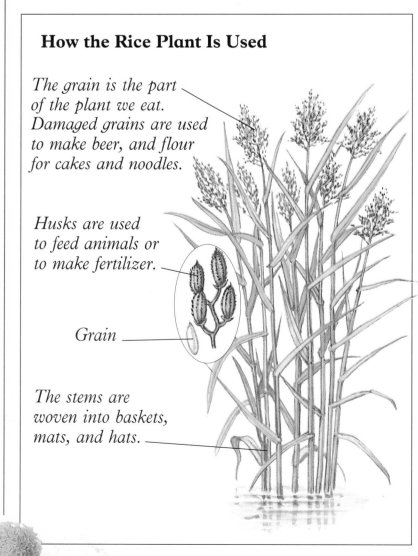

The grain is the part of the plant we eat. Damaged grains are used to make beer, and flour for cakes and noodles.

Husks are used to feed animals or to make fertilizer.

Grain

The stems are woven into baskets, mats, and hats.

Preparing the Fields
The paddy fields are flooded, plowed, raked, and flattened. In Asia, buffaloes are used to do the heavy work.

Planting Out
The seedlings, grown earlier, are moved to the paddy fields. They are planted in straight lines and given plenty of space to grow.

While water helps the rice grow, it kills off weeds that can't grow in such wet conditions.

Rice is a type of grass.

Most rice is grown in flooded fields, called paddies.

The fields are flooded for much of the growing season.

The rice is planted in straight lines.

Machine Power

In the United States, growing rice is highly mechanized. Tractors prepare the fields. The seed may be sown from airplanes. Combine harvesters gather the ripe plants.

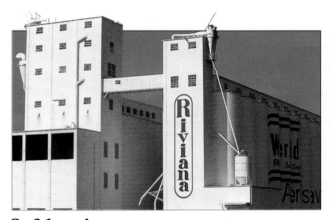

Safekeeping

Special buildings are used to store the rice until it is needed. They are called granaries. A granary keeps the grain dry and safe from hungry animals.

All Rice

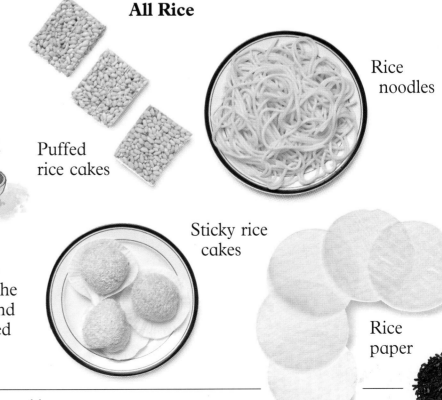

Puffed rice cakes

Rice noodles

Sticky rice cakes

Rice paper

Harvesting

The rice is ready for harvesting in three to six months. The fields are drained and the plants cut down, tied in bundles, and left to dry.

Winnowing

The rice is beaten to remove the grains. The grains are crushed and then sieved and tossed to remove any fine pieces of husk.

BEANS AND PEAS

This is soy milk. It is made from soybeans and is useful for people who cannot drink cow's milk.

Peas, beans, and lentils are all pulses – edible seeds that grow in a pod on a plant. Some, such as green peas and fava beans, are usually eaten fresh; others, such as white kidney beans and adzuki beans, are dried. Pulses are packed with the protein and vitamins we need to keep healthy. In some parts of the world, people get their protein from fish, eggs, and meat. But for people in many developing countries, peas, beans, and lentils are an excellent alternative and are a staple in their diet.

Dal is an Indian dish made with lentils. Many people in India are forbidden by their religion to eat meat, so pulses are an important part of their diet.

Chili con carne is a spicy dish of meat and red kidney beans from Mexico.

Sekihan, or red rice, is a Japanese dish in which red beans are mixed with rice to color it pink.

Kidney beans are mixed with vegetables to make this bean burger. It is an alternative to a hamburger.

Piles of Pulses

Most beans, lentils, and peas are dried after harvesting so they will keep for a long time. Dried pulses must be soaked in water before cooking.

Red kidney beans

Flageolet beans

Adzuki beans

Orange lentils

Split green peas

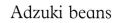

Tofu looks like a soft cheese, but is really a curd made from soybeans. It is used a lot in Chinese cooking.

These Chinese moon cakes are filled with a sugary paste made from adzuki beans.

When you eat these fresh green beans and peas, you eat the pods, too.

Rice mixed with peas makes a nutritious dish.

The Wonder Bean
Soybeans grow where there is sun but no frost. They are richer in protein than meat. They can also be made into margarine, flour, oil, and powdered baby milk.

Juicy Shoots
If mung beans are soaked in water, they will sprout shoots in just a few days. These shoots are good to eat, both raw and cooked.

Dried mung beans

Tiny shoots appear.

Mung bean sprouts

Surprise, Surprise!
Peanuts are not nuts, but peas! Like peas, they grow in pods, but peanut pods grow under the ground. After flowering, the stem withers and then falls to the ground, where the tip swells to form a pod. Peanuts are grown chiefly for their oil.

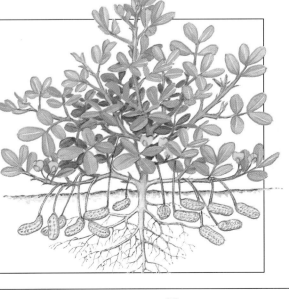

VEGETABLE OILS

Vegetable oils are made from the seeds and fruits of many plants growing all over the world, from tiny sesame seeds to big, juicy coconuts. The oils are used for cooking, as salad dressings, and in margarine and cooking fats. Soybeans are the most important source of oil worldwide, especially in the United States. In western Europe, the oil most widely produced is rapeseed oil.

Harvesting
Olives are picked in the autumn when they are ripe. They are shaken from the trees and gathered up, usually by hand. Next, the olives are sorted out to remove the leaves and twigs and taken to be pressed.

Olive trees are often quite small, but can live for hundreds of years. They develop very wrinkled, knotty trunks.

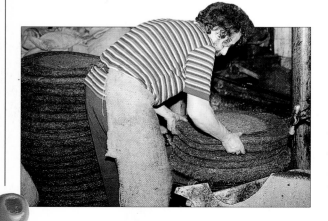

How Olive Oil Is Made
The olives are ground into a thick paste, which is spread onto special mats. The mats are then layered up on the pressing machine, which will gently squeeze them to produce olive oil.

Olive trees are planted in rows. Fields of olive trees are called groves.

Edible Olives

There are many varieties of olives – black and green, large and small. Most are used for making oil, but some are eaten whole, too. Raw olives are very bitter, but once they have been treated, fermented, and pickled, they taste delicious!

Surprising Sources

Oil can be produced from lots of very different fruits and seeds.

Peanuts

Cottonseeds

Sesame seeds

The trees are shaken to make the olives fall. Sometimes, machines are used to do this job.

Each long, flexible branch has lots of flowers and about 30 clusters of fruit.

Rapeseed

Soybeans

Sunflower Oil

Every sunflower is made up of hundreds of tiny flowers surrounded by a fringe of petals. It is the seeds of the flowers that are rich in oil. Sunflowers are ready for harvesting when the flowers are dead and the heads have dried out. Sunflower oil is good for making cooking oil, salad oil, and margarine.

Nets are laid down so that the fallen fruit can be gathered easily.

CATTLE AND DAIRY FARMING

Cattle are very popular domesticated animals because they provide us with a lot of food. They are kept for their meat, which is called beef, and also for their milk. Because milk contains a wide range of vital nutrients, such as calcium, protein, and carbohydrates, milk-giving animals are kept all over the world – but they are not always cows. Goats, sheep, camels, reindeer, and llamas give us milk, too!

A cow gives milk for ten months of the year. Then she has a rest for two months. Most cows are milked twice a day.

To produce milk, a dairy cow must have a calf once a year.

Milky Ways
To make just 1 pound (about half a kilogram) of butter, you need a little over 2.5 gallons (9.8 liters) of milk. The leftover liquid is called buttermilk.

A calf born to a dairy cow stays with its mother for just 48 hours.

The Big Cheese
Foods made from milk, like butter, cheese, yogurt, and cream, are known as dairy products. Making cheese is the best way to turn milk into a food that can be stored for some time. Thousands of different cheeses are made all over the world. Soft, creamy cheeses must be eaten promptly, but hard, crumbly cheeses will last for months and even years!

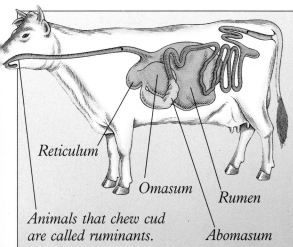

Reticulum

Omasum

Rumen

Abomasum

Animals that chew cud are called ruminants.

Second Helping

Cows eat grass without chewing it properly. It goes to the rumen and reticulum to be broken down into cud. The cow sucks this up and chews it again. When it is swallowed, the cud goes through the stomachs in turn, finally being digested in the abomasum.

Dairy Cattle

Holstein-friesian

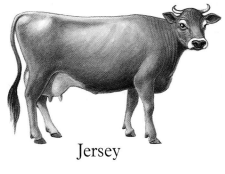

Jersey

This is the udder, where the milk is produced. It is in four parts. Each part has a teat.

In the Milking Parlor

When cows are milked, special suckers are attached to the teats. They squeeze the milk gently from the cow just as a calf does. Most cows give about 3 gallons (11.5 liters) of milk per day.

Beef Cattle

Hereford

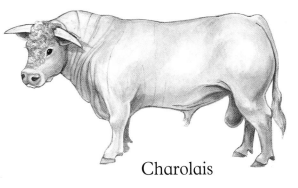

Charolais

Bred for Beef

Big, heavy breeds of cattle are kept for beef because they have more meat on them. The world's largest herds of beef cattle are found in North and South America. Here there are lots of wide, open spaces where the cattle can graze until they are fat and ready for eating.

Dairy and Beef

Simmental

SHEEP

Sheep are raised for their meat, for the foods that can be made from their milk, and for their wool. There are over 200 breeds of sheep and different kinds are able to live in very different places – in lands that are hot with little water, in areas that are cold and wet, in the lowlands, and on the hills. The kind of place where it lives affects the quality of the sheep's meat and wool.

Sheep Produce

Sheep provide milk, yogurt, and cheese, and wool for clothing. The wool contains a fat, called lanolin. It is used in ointments and hand creams.

Lanolin

Yogurt

Cheese

Milk

It takes the wool from one average-size fleece to make this sweater.

An experienced shearer can shear a great many sheep in one day. At shearing time, shearers travel from farm to farm to clip the animals.

Hand-operated shears or electric clippers are used by the shearer.

Sheep are shorn in the spring and early summer when they no longer need their long coats to keep them warm.

The fleece is made into wool for knitting and for making carpets and fabrics. Sometimes, it is even used to fill mattresses.

Bath Time
Once or twice a year, the farmer drives the sheep through a chemical dip. This keeps them free of pests and diseases.

Domestic Sheep

Suffolk

Mommy!
Some lambs are orphaned or not wanted by their mom. These may be bottle-fed by the farmer or shepherd or adopted by another ewe.

Wensleydale

Working Dogs
Dogs are used to gather the sheep in flocks and move them from place to place. Sheepdogs naturally like to herd animals, but they need to be trained to follow instructions. The shepherd controls the dog using special calls and whistles. Sheep are timid, so the dog will run low in the grass to avoid frightening them.

Karakul

In a Spin
To produce wool for knitting or weaving, many strands are twisted together to make one long thread. Spinning was first done by hand using a spindle. Later, the spindle was attached to a wheel, and wool could be spun more quickly. Now, most spinning is done by machine.

Scottish blackface

Wild Sheep

Bighorn

The shearer shears the sheep so that the fleece comes off in one piece.

PIGS

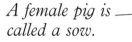
Duroc

Domestic pigs are mainly kept for their meat, especially in China, which has the most pigs in the world. Pigs raised for their meat are usually kept in pens and are fed on cereals, potatoes, fish meal, and skimmed milk. Pigs kept for breeding often live outdoors in fields. The farmer feeds them, but they also search for their own food. They like worms, snails, roots, and plants.

Mud, Glorious Mud
Despite their reputation, pigs are not dirty animals. They cannot sweat, so in hot weather they roll about in mud to help cool themselves down.

A female pig is called a sow.

Intensive Farming
When pigs leave their mothers, they are normally housed in piggeries. This is so they can be looked after properly and kept warm. The pigs are fed a special diet, and because they have less space to run around, they put on weight quickly.

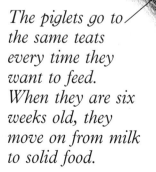

The piglets go to the same teats every time they want to feed. When they are six weeks old, they move on from milk to solid food.

A sow makes a "nest" before she has her litter. In a pen, she paws straw into a heap. In a field, she lines a hole with leaves and straw.

20

Pig Parade

Landrace

British saddleback

Piétrain

Vietnamese potbellied pig

Domestic pigs don't have hairy coats to protect them, just a few short bristles. Because of this, pink pigs can get sunburned. Black pigs are protected by their dark skins.

Pig Products

The meat from pigs is used to make a variety of foods, including sausages, all kinds of hams, and spiced meats.

The last piglet born is often smaller and weaker than the rest. It is called the "runt," and it may not live.

Detective Work

Pigs have a good sense of smell and use their snouts to dig up food. In France, pigs are used to search for truffles, which are difficult to find because they can grow as much as 12 inches (30 centimeters) underground.

Truffles are like mushrooms and are a great delicacy.

A sow usually has about 10 to 12 piglets in a litter. She can have more than two litters every year.

GOATS

In many parts of the world where the land is too scrubby, too hot, or too steep to raise cattle and sheep, farmers often keep goats instead. These hardy animals thrive in difficult countryside and are not too choosy about what they eat. They provide meat, milk, and dairy products. Some kinds of goats are also kept for their fiber, or hair, and for their skins.

Open Wide!
Like sheep and cattle, goats have a hard pad on the top jaw, not teeth.

All goats, male and female, can have horns, although some breeds do not grow them.

Goats usually have coats of thick, coarse hair.

Getting Goats Going
Goats can easily live where the climate is very hot and dry. These goats are being herded along a dried-up riverbed in Kenya, Africa.

The hooves have a hard rim and a soft inner sole. They act like suction cups when the goat leaps from rock to rock.

The udder of a milking goat has two teats. The goats are milked twice a day.

Goats will stand up on their hind legs to reach branches and leaves.

Goat Products

Milk

Yogurt

Cheese

Leafy Wrapping
Cheese must be wrapped
to keep it from drying out.

Scaling the Heights
Mountain goats are creatures of the
heights. They are surefooted and
have a good sense of balance. They
can walk along narrow ledges and
leap from one high cliff to another.

Various Breeds

Pygmy goat

Cashmere

Saanen

Anglo-Nubian

Value Added
This is an Angora goat. Its coat is
very valuable. When shorn, the
long, shiny, all-white ringlets of
fiber, called mohair, can be made
into expensive knitwear. Other
luxury fabrics made from goat's fiber
are called cashmere and cashgora (a mixture
of cashmere and angora). An angora goat can
grow 1 inch (2.5 cm) of mohair in a month.

Buck or billy

Nanny

Kid

All in the Family
Male goats are called billies or
bucks. The females are nannies,
and the babies are kids.

POULTRY

This is a free-range chicken. It is allowed plenty of room to run about outside.

Farmers keep poultry for their meat and for their eggs. The birds are so popular that people all over the world eat about 30 million tons of their meat each year and about the same weight in eggs. Poultry are chickens, geese, turkeys, ducks, guinea fowl, and pigeons. In some places, poultry also includes peacocks and peahens, which are kept for their meat, and ostriches, which are kept for their eggs, meat, and hides.

Guinea fowl

Chickens lay most of their eggs in their first year. They are usually sold for their meat in their second year.

When the chicks are five months old, they will be ready to lay eggs themselves.

Fine Feathers

Ducklings as well as ducks are raised for their meat. Ducks also provide soft feathers, called down, for filling quilts.

Healthy Appetites

Turkeys eat a lot and grow very quickly. They can put on about one pound (half a kilogram) a week.

The chicks learn what to eat from their mother. They do this by pecking whatever she pecks.

Home Sweet Home

Hens need shelter and protection from animals such as foxes. Free-range birds usually have a special house that can be moved with them as they are transferred from field to field.

Production Line

In a battery, thousands of hens are kept in separate cages stacked up in a large building. They are kept in artificial light, which encourages them to lay more eggs. Their food and water are fed to them automatically.

Exotic Dish

In some parts of India, domestic peacocks and peahens are raised for their meat.

Inside the Egg

Most eggs are not fertilized and won't turn into chicks. To produce chicks, a hen must be mated with a rooster. Eggs provide food and shelter for any developing chick inside.

Shell

This spot on the yolk may develop into a chick.

The yolk is the chick's food supply.

The egg white contains water for the chick.

Twisted cords keep the yolk in the middle of the egg.

Free-range chickens use their claws to scratch for food, usually worms and seeds. The farmer will also give them grain.

FISHING

The rivers, seas, and oceans are a rich source of fish, shellfish, and even sea vegetables, such as seaweed! Most of the fish we eat come from the sea, but fish can also be raised on farms, just like other animals. Salmon and trout are popular fish to farm, but other types, including turbot, sole, and plaice, are kept, too. Inland, the fish are kept in ponds or tanks. At sea, or in lochs, the fish are kept in cages.

Shellfish Farming
Shellfish can be farmed, too. These mussels are growing on wooden posts. They can also be grown on ropes. When fully grown, they are easy to pick at low tide.

Convenience Food
At feeding time on the fish farm, the water swirls with hungry fish. The farmer feeds fish eggs or very young fish to the growing fish. Because they don't have to use up energy hunting for their own food, the fish put on weight very quickly.

Floating Factories
Some big fishing ships go to sea for as long as three months at a time. Because of this, the fish must be prepared and stored on board. These ships hold such a lot of people and equipment that they are called factory ships.

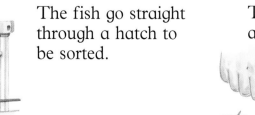

The fish go straight through a hatch to be sorted.

The fish are gutted and cleaned.

Packed like Sardines

Fish do not stay fresh for very long, and this catch must be preserved as soon as possible. A popular way to preserve fish such as sardines is to can them with oil. Because there is no air in the can, they will stay fresh for a long time.

The Fisher's Catch

There are several types of fish and seafood. Creatures with hard bodies, such as clams and crabs, are called shellfish. Herrings are oily fish. They have more fat in them than white fish, such as cod. River or pond fish, such as trout, are freshwater fish.

Littleneck clams

Crab

Herring

Up in Smoke

These herrings are hanging in a room with very gently burning wood chips. This will smoke them, which gives the fish a good flavor and helps to preserve them. Salmon and eels are also popular smoked fish.

Cod

They are divided into fillets.

The fillets are stored in huge deepfreezes.

Trout

When the ship returns to port, the boxes of frozen fish are unloaded.

TREE FRUITS

Fruits grown on trees come in many different forms. They may be firm and crisp like apples, soft and juicy like peaches, or crunchy like nuts. In temperate climates, apples are one of the most widely grown fruits. To keep the trees healthy and to produce the best crop, the apple grower has different tasks to do in the orchards every season.

Inside an Apple
The flesh of an apple protects the seeds as they begin to grow.

The stalk attaches the apple to the tree.

The seeds, or pips, are inside a tough core.

Summer
In summer, the trees are pruned to get sunlight to the apples to ripen them. They are sprayed to protect them from pests and fed with fertilizers to help produce a good crop.

The earth around the trees is kept bare to free the trees from weeds.

Modern fruit trees are small. This makes the fruit easy to pick.

Nuts
The part of the nut you eat is called the kernel. It is the seed of the plant. Nuts are nourishing. They are used in a variety of dishes and also to make oils.

Coconut

Brazil nuts grow inside a round, hard fruit. Some of the fruits can be as large as a human head.

Brazil

Coconut flesh is eaten fresh, or dried and used in cakes and sweets.

Pecan

Pistachio

The apples are picked by hand, starting in late summer.

Stone Fruits

In some fruits, the seed is protected by a hard shell, called the stone.

| Cherry | Greengage | Plum | Nectarine |

The trees are grown in rows to make mechanical weeding and feeding easy to do.

The pickers put the apples into small containers. When the containers are full, they are emptied into large wooden bins.

The bins are moved by tractor or forklift.

Hands On

Apple trees are pruned and trained into different shapes to make the fruit easy to reach. The spindlebush has ropes to pull the branches down.

| Pyramid | Standard | Spindlebush |

Autumn

Apple picking continues. Windfalls are collected to make cider and juice. Some may be fed to livestock.

Winter

In winter, the trees take a rest from growing. During this season, the trees are pruned again to shape them.

Spring

The trees are sprayed, fed, and pruned. Beehives may be put in the orchards because insects are needed to pollinate the blossoms.

CITRUS FRUITS

The ugli fruit is a cross between a tangerine, an orange, and a grapefruit

The third largest fruit crop in the world, after grapes and bananas, is citrus fruits. This is the family of fruits that oranges, lemons, and satsumas all belong to. Citrus fruits are grown mainly in tropical and subtropical parts of North and South America, in northern and eastern Mediterranean countries, and in Australia.

A tree can produce a thousand oranges each year.

This is a white grapefruit. The flesh inside is a pale yellow.

Lemons, like other citrus fruits, are rich in minerals and vitamins, especially vitamin C.

Tangerines are like small, sweet oranges. They have several small pips.

Limes have thin skins and very sharp juice.

Fighting Frost

Citrus trees need just the right climate to produce good fruit – sun to make them sweet and then cold to make them sharp. But the trees' greatest enemy is frost, which will kill the fruit. So modern plantations often have wind machines and special orchard heaters in case it is frosty.

Orchard heaters protect the trees from frost.

This is a pink grapefruit. Inside, it has a sweet, pink flesh.

The Perfect Package
Citrus fruits are perfectly packaged foods. In the middle is the juicy flesh, a wonderful source of food and drink that is rich in vitamin C. Next comes a spongy layer, called the pith, which cushions the flesh. On the outside is a protective skin.

Tough skin

Soft flesh

Pith

Navel oranges are very juicy. Usually they have no seeds.

Clementines, like satsumas and tangerines, have a loose skin that is easy to peel.

Satsumas are like tangerines, except they don't have pips.

You can eat kumquats whole, including the rind.

Mix and Match
By mixing pollen from the blossoms of different citrus trees, new varieties can be developed. The limequat, for example, is a cross between a lime and a kumquat.

Juicy Fruit
These oranges are being sorted and packed and will be sold for eating. Many oranges are pulped to be made into juice. This pulp is frozen for transporting around the world.

Fresh orange juice contains the most goodness, so squeeze it yourself if you can.

31

GRAPES

There are two different types of grapes: black and white. But black grapes are really dark red, and white grapes are light green. Grapes are delicious to eat fresh and keep their sweetness when dried, too. But most of the grapes grown in the world are used for making wine. Grape plants are called vines. They are planted in rows in vineyards. Vines need a lot of care, and it takes much hard work and skill to produce a bottle of fine wine.

Grapes need rain to swell them and sun to ripen them.

The broad vine leaves shade the grapes from the direct glare of the sun and the battering rain.

Pruning

As vines grow, they are often cut back so they have a few strong branches rather than lots of weaker ones. This work is called pruning and must be done by hand.

Bitter Wine

Red and white wine can also be made into vinegar. It is produced when special vinegar yeasts ferment the wine and turn it sour. Vinegars can be made from other liquids, such as cider or malt, and are used as a flavoring. They can also be mixed with foods to pickle and preserve them.

From Grapes to Wine

First the grapes are crushed and pressed to mix the yeast with the sugar in the grapes. This is called fermentation. Then the juice is filtered and poured into vats. These are left in a cool place for the flavor of the wine to develop.

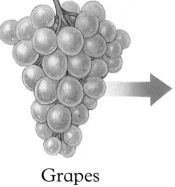

Grapes

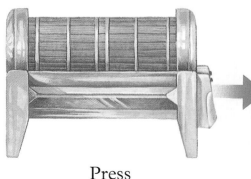

Press

There is a natural yeast on the grape skin that is needed to turn the grape juice into wine.

Black grapes can be made into red or white wine. To make red wine, the skins of black grapes are left in the wine mixture.

Grapes grow in tight bunches.

Dried Goods

Grapes for drying must be very sweet because it is their natural sugar that preserves them. They can be dried on racks, in the sun, or in ovens. Only seedless grapes are used for drying. Sultanas are dried white grapes. Raisins and currants are dried black grapes and are usually smaller.

Currants

Raisins

Sultanas

Grape Harvesters

Most wine grapes today are picked by machine, except in small or sloping vineyards. Special grapes for making rare wines are carefully picked by hand.

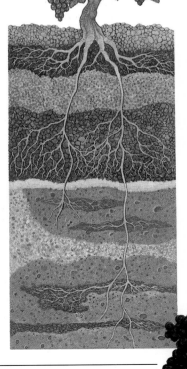

Digging Deep

The type of soil in a vineyard is very important and affects the flavor of the wine. Yet some of the best wines are produced from poor soils. This is because the vine can find regular supplies of food and water by pushing its roots deep into the earth.

Vats

Wine

TROPICAL FRUITS

When you eat an exotic fruit such as a banana or a pineapple, do you ever wonder where it came from and how it got to you? Exotic fruits come from the tropics, where the climate is hot and wet. Tropical fruits are full of vitamins, minerals, and the fiber needed for a healthy diet, but they are delicate and don't keep well. You are able to eat them fresh even though they have traveled thousands of miles because they are transported in ships and trucks that are specially cooled.

The leaves can be 12 feet (3.5 meters) long.

Finger Food
The bananas grow along the stem of the flower. The separate fruits are called fingers. There may be 50 to 150 separate fruits in a bunch. They are grouped in "hands" of 10 to 20.

Bananas are high in carbohydrates, mainly as sugar. They are high in vitamins A and C and low in fat and protein. They also contain potassium.

The flower grows out of the middle of the trunk.

The "trunk" grows 10 to 20 ft (3 to 6 m) high.

The banana plant looks like a palm tree, but it isn't a tree. Its trunk is made of leaves, not wood and bark.

Now You See Them . . .

The banana plants growing on this plantation look as though they will be as long-lived as the trees of a forest. In fact, they die once they have fruited. They are replaced by new plants that grow from the underground stem of the first plant.

Out of the Ordinary

Exotic fruits may have strange shapes, be brightly colored, and have very unusual textures inside.

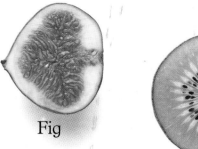

Lychee

Fig

Kiwifruit

Cape gooseberry

Travel Packs

Bananas are one of the world's most important crops. They are a staple in the tropics and are exported all over the world. They are picked and packed when they are still hard and green.

Passion fruit

Star fruit, or carambola

A Canny Idea

Canning is a way of preserving fresh food and keeping it from going bad. When pineapple is canned, it is cut into chunks or rings. Next, the fruit is put into cans and topped up with syrup or fruit juice. The cans are sealed to make them airtight, heated, and then cooled.

Mango

Papaya, or pawpaw

UNDERGROUND VEGETABLES

Some plants are not grown for their leafy tops but for the parts of them that grow beneath the soil. Carrots, turnips, radishes, and parsnips are the fat roots of plants and are known as root vegetables. Potatoes are the swollen part of the underground stem of the plant. They are called tubers. Onions, too, grow in the dark earth, but it is the bulb of these plants that we eat.

The flowers produce seeds, which can be used to grow new plants, but it is more common to use seed potatoes.

Farming with Nature

Many farmers use chemical fertilizers and pesticides to help them grow crops efficiently, but some farmers use only natural products. They use fertilizers such as manure and encourage pest controllers such as ladybugs, which eat all sorts of flies and larvae. This helps to stop a buildup of chemicals in the environment and is called organic farming.

Potato plants grow well in cool climates, but are killed by frost.

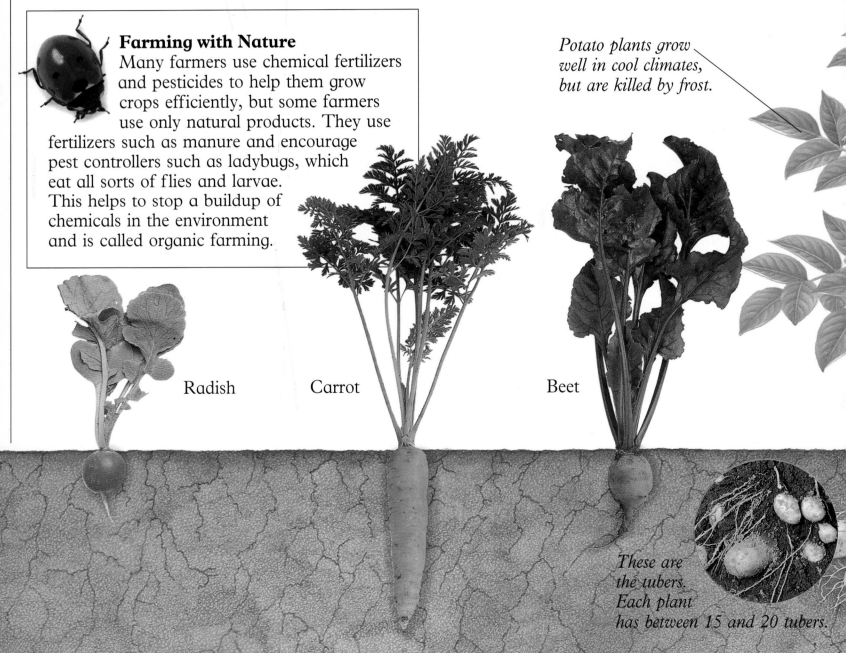

Radish

Carrot

Beet

These are the tubers. Each plant has between 15 and 20 tubers.

Types of Tubers
Tubers come in all shapes and sizes.

Sweet potato

Cassava

Yam

Cocoyam

Harvest Time
In the autumn, the potatoes are fully grown, and special harvesters, pulled by tractors, are used to lift them carefully from the soil.

When the leaves wither in the autumn, the farmer knows the potatoes are ready to harvest.

Tasty Bulbs
Bulbs, such as onions, are not roots. Instead, they are made up of clumps of tightly curled leaves. Leeks, garlic, shallots, and spring onions are all members of the same plant family, and they are all valuable for the flavor that they can give to many other foods.

Garlic

Shallot

— *Stem*

Some potatoes may be harvested and put to one side. These will then be used to grow new plants and are called seed potatoes.

Onion

From these tiny scars, called eyes, new shoots will grow.

Roots

HOTHOUSE VEGETABLES

In countries with cool climates, there is not usually enough heat to grow delicate or tropical vegetables. But in special hothouses with glass or clear plastic walls, a farmer can grow almost any crop. This is because the temperature inside a hothouse can be controlled. Hothouses are useful in warm countries, too. They free the farmer from having to follow the seasons, and summer vegetables that do not store well can be grown fresh all year round.

Computer Controlled
Tomatoes are quite fragile plants, so this hothouse, where the temperature and feeding are controlled by a computer, is a good place to grow them. Tomatoes grown in hothouses are usually top quality and are picked by hand.

Nature's "Hothouse"
Some of the world's hottest spots are dry deserts. But if a water supply can be set up, the desert heat can be put to good use. Fertile gardens can be created, such as this fruit orchard in Jordan.

Short Showers
Most of the work in large hothouses today is done by machines. The young sweet-pepper plants shown above are watered by overhead pipes. Hothouse crops must also be sprayed to protect them from the pests and molds that like the damp, warm conditions.

A Carpet of Seedlings

Seeds germinate quickly in the warmth and protection of the hothouse. These are lettuce seedlings. Hothouses can be large, and some are half the size of a football field.

Water Gardens

Some vegetables can be grown without soil. The plants are carefully supported and supplied with water that is automatically mixed with plant foods. This way of growing plants is called hydroponics.

This material does not feed the plants, but helps to support them.

Water full of plant food flows past the roots.

Mixed Vegetables

Here are some other vegetables that would normally need lots of sun to grow, but can be farmed in hothouses in cool climates.

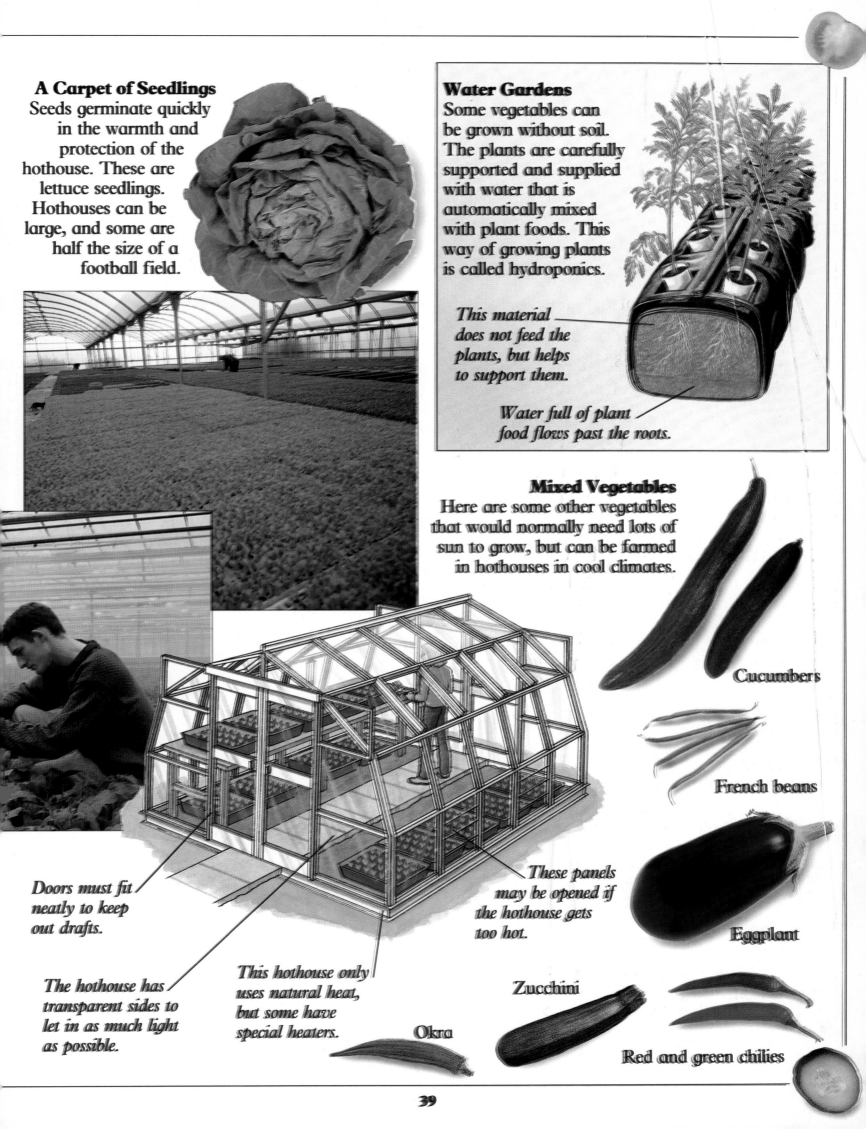

Cucumbers

French beans

Eggplant

Zucchini

Okra

Red and green chilies

Doors must fit neatly to keep out drafts.

These panels may be opened if the hothouse gets too hot.

The hothouse has transparent sides to let in as much light as possible.

This hothouse only uses natural heat, but some have special heaters.

SPICES AND HERBS

Spices and herbs do not make a meal in themselves, but they give many of our everyday foods a lot of flavor. Spices come from many parts of different plants – seeds, bark, leaves, nuts, berries, and buds.

Herbs are usually the leaves or the flowers of plants. Both spices and herbs can be used fresh or dried.

Cloves are dried buds. The heads can be ground into a powder.

This is fresh gingerroot. It is also used dried.

Paprika is made from ground, sweet red peppers.

These fresh chilies are red because they have been left to ripen.

Cinnamon sticks are made from the dried bark of a tree.

Cardamom is one of the world's most costly spices. In the Middle East, it is added to coffee.

A nutmeg is the nut inside a fruit rather like an apricot.

Curry leaves are best used fresh because they lose most of their flavor when dried.

Coriander seeds

Pots of Pepper

Peppercorns can be pink, black, green, or white, but they are all the berries of the same plant. The color varies depending on when the peppercorns are harvested and how they are treated. For instance, black peppercorns are green when picked, but change color when dried.

A Touch of Spice

These are just a few examples of foods that get their flavor from spices.

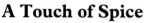

Hot red-pepper sauce

Caraway cheese

Mustard

Gingerbread

Saffron bun

Just a Pinch
Spices usually come from tropical plants. They are used in small amounts, whole or ground.

Turmeric is mainly used to give food a yellow color.

Fields of Flavor
This is a colorful crop of borage, an herb that is used in salads and drinks. Herbs are farmed on a large scale just like other foods. Some are sold for use in cooking, and some are sold to industry to make products such as soap.

Fenugreek seeds are dried before being ground into a powder.

Dried red chilies

These chilies are green because they are unripe.

Nutmegs are surrounded by a lacy covering. This makes a spice called mace.

Allspice is made by grinding these berries into a powder.

Cayenne pepper is made from a type of red chili pepper.

Cumin seeds have a hot, bitter flavor. They are used in curries.

A Handful of Herbs
Many herbs have wonderful smells, as well as tastes. Some are used to make teas or even medicines.

Applemint

Parsley

Sage

Rosemary

Thyme

Spice Land
Spices are very important to India. Of all the countries in the world, it exports the most. This woman is sifting ground spices. Many spices are very hard, so we buy them already ground.

COFFEE, TEA, AND COCOA

Coffee, tea, and cocoa are drunk in most countries of the world. Cocoa is also used to make chocolate. Coffee and cocoa grow in the tropics. They are grown on huge plantations, but a lot is produced on small farms as well. Tea is grown in the tropics and subtropics, on plantations. Altogether, millions of people are employed to produce these crops. Coffee, tea, and cocoa are important to the countries that grow them because they are cash crops. This means they are grown to be traded with other countries rather than for home use.

Picky Pickers

Tea comes from evergreen trees that are pruned into bushes. This makes it easy to pick the leaves. The best quality teas are produced by plucking only the bud and the first two leaves on each shoot. A skilled plucker can pick enough leaves in one day to make 3,500 cups of tea.

Green tea   Black tea

Special Treatment

The leaves are made into green or black tea. For green tea, the leaves are dried, heated, and crushed. For black tea, the leaves are dried, crushed, fermented, and dried again.

A coffee tree produces about 2,000 fruits each year. It takes half this amount to make just one pound (half a kilogram) of roasted coffee.

The fruits are called cherries because of their color and size.

There are two green coffee beans inside each cherry. They only turn brown after they are roasted.

The coffee is harvested twice a year.

The trees are pruned to keep them from growing more than ten feet (three meters) high.

When the fruits first appear, they are green. Gradually, they turn bright red. They are then ready to be picked.

The ripe fruit is picked by hand or shaken from the tree onto a cloth spread out underneath it. On some plantations, machines are used to pick the fruit.

Heavy Load

Cocoa pods are large and heavy. They grow on the trunk of the cacao tree or from its thick branches.

The pod has a thick skin.

Each pod may contain 20 to 50 cocoa beans.

The pod grows up to 15 inches (38 centimeters) long, a few inches longer than a football.

SUGAR

Most people like sugar. Nearly 100 million tons of it are produced each year. Over half of it comes from sugarcane. This is grown on a large scale on plantations in the tropical areas of Brazil, Cuba, India, China, Australia, Mexico, the Philippines, Thailand, and the United States. The rest of our sugar comes from sugar beet, which is a vegetable. This grows in the cooler climates of Europe, the United States, Canada, China, and Japan.

Workers Watch Out!
The sugar plantations can be home to the deadly bushmaster snake. Enormous bird-eating spiders also nestle among the thick foliage.

Sugarcane
Sugarcane is a tropical plant. It grows best in places that get plenty of sunshine and lots of rain.

The canes are cut close to the ground because this is where the most sugar collects.

Sugarcane is a very tall grass, like rice and cereals.

The sugar is stored inside the stalk in a firm pulp.

The stalks of a mature plant are about two inches (five centimeters) thick.

After the cane has been harvested, healthy stumps will regrow into new plants.

Sugar Beet
Sugar beet is a root vegetable. It looks like a giant parsnip. It grows best in places that have warm summers and cool or cold winters.

The leafy tops of the plants are cut off before the sugar beet is lifted. The tops can be used for animal feed.

The sugar is stored in the thick root.

The canes are cut when they are 13 to 17 feet (4 to 5 m) high.

The canes are ripe when they look dry.

Sugar Production

In a sugar factory, sugar from the canes or beets is taken out, cleaned, and boiled. This leaves a syrup, which turns into brown sugar crystals. These can be refined to make white sugar.

Sorts of Sugar

Sugars differ in color and in the size of their crystals, or grains.

Granulated

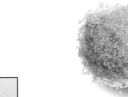

Turbinado

Dark brown

Muscovado

Sugarcane is often harvested by machine, but in some places it is still cut by hand.

Maple Syrup

Maple syrup is made from the sap of sugar maple or black maple trees. Holes are made in the trunks in winter, when the trees are dormant. When a thaw follows a freeze, the sap runs and is collected from the wounds in buckets. Maple syrup is produced only in North America.

FEEDING THE WORLD

Every year, the world's population goes up and up. By the year 2020, there could be as many as 7 billion people in the world. Millions do not have enough to eat now, so how will the world cope in the future? Some of the answers could come from changing ways of farming to give us more food. More land could be farmed by improving the watering of dry land and by getting back land from the sea. New crops could be developed, and new animals domesticated.

Two for One
Two or more crops can be planted together to help each other grow. When corn and beans are planted together in the same field, the corn supports the bean plants, while the bean plants fix nitrogen in the soil and help make it fertile.

Two for the Price of One
In China, the rice growers often keep ducks or fish in the flooded paddy fields. This means that two foods come from the same piece of land.

Greening the Land

In some places, there isn't enough rain for crops to grow. This can be changed if artificial ways are found to water the land. The Imperial Valley in California, shown here, used to be parched desert.

Crops of the Future

Another way to produce more food is to grow crops that can live in difficult conditions.

Yam

Job's tears

Winged bean

Stepping Up Production

In hilly or mountainous areas, the land is cut into terraces. This means that there is more land for growing crops. Terracing also helps stop the soil from being blown away by wind or washed away by rains.

Easy to Please

Deer are animals that can live on poor land and still produce good meat. Because of this, some kinds of deer have been domesticated and are being kept on farms.

Breadfruit

GLOSSARY

Cash crop A crop that is grown to be sold rather than used by the farmer.

Cereals Grains that you can eat, such as wheat, barley, sweet corn, and rice.

Citrus fruits The family of fruits that includes oranges, lemons, and grapefruits.

Combine harvester A large harvesting machine that not only cuts wheat, but also separates the grain from the straw.

Crop rotation A way of farming to help keep the soil from losing its goodness by changing the type of crop grown in a field each year.

Evergreen A plant or tree that constantly loses and grows new leaves throughout the year.

Factory ship A large fishing ship that has all the equipment needed to prepare, store, can, or freeze the fish it catches.

Fermentation This is what happens when food is broken down by yeast or bacteria. Wine, cheese, and yogurt are all foods made by fermentation.

Fertilizer Something that is added to soil to help plants grow. There are natural fertilizers, such as animal manure, and also human-made chemical fertilizers.

Free-range Farm animals that are given freedom to move around.

Granaries Large buildings that are used for storing grains and cereals.

Husk A dry, thin covering that protects seeds or grains.

Hydroponics A way of growing plants in a mixture of water and chemicals instead of soil.

Irrigation The use of canals, water pipes, or wells to water land that needs a special water supply.

Kernel A seed found inside a hard covering, like a nut.

Locust An insect, rather like a grasshopper, that eats plants. They live in huge swarms and are a terrible threat to crops.

Paddy field A field that is flooded for growing rice.

Pesticides Chemicals that are used to control pests that attack crops.

Plantation A large farm, usually in a hot country, where only one type of crop is grown.

Pollen A powder found in seed-making plants that is important for growing fruits and vegetables.

Poultry Birds, such as chickens, turkeys, ducks, and geese, that are kept for their eggs or meat.

Reclaimed land An area of land that at one time could not be used because it was a desert or under the sea, but that people have managed to turn into fertile farmland.

Staple foods The basic foods that are eaten all over a particular area. A staple food of China, for example, is rice.

Terracing Cutting sloping land into steps so that it can be used for farming.

Tropics Areas of the world where the climate is very hot, usually with heavy rainfall. Areas where the climate is slightly less hot and less wet are called subtropical areas.

Tuber A swollen underground stem, such as a potato.

Vineyard A field where grape vines are planted in rows.

Windfalls Ripe tree fruits that have been blown to the ground by the wind.

Winnowing The beating of cereals to separate the grain from the husk.

Yeast A fungus that grows very quickly when mixed with sugar. Yeast is used to make bread and wine.

Acknowledgments

Photography: Andy Crawford, Chris King, Steve Gorton, Ray Moller, Tim Ridley, Dave Rudkin.
Additional Photography: Steve Bartholomew, Jane Burton, Geoff Dann, Philip Dowell, Dave King, David Murray, Martin Norris, Stephen Oliver, Susanna Price, Matthew Ward.
Illustrations: Graham Allen, Roy Flooks, Charlotte Hard, Stuart Lafford, Steve Lings, Josephine Martin, Sean Milne, Liz Pepperell, Gill Platt, Pete Serjeant, Clive Spong. Phil Weare.
Thanks to: Francesca Baines, Caroline Brooke, Donks Models, Mark Lamey at Kew Gardens, Wendy Lee, Scallywags models.

Picture credits

Heather Angel: 42cb; **Bruce Coleman Ltd.:** John Cancalosi 9cl, Giuliano Cappelli 33cr, Christer Fredriksson 22clb, Steven C. Kaufman 47cb, Stephen J. Krasemann 17cb, M.Timothy O'Keefe 30cb, Dr. Eckart Pott 15br, Dr. Sandro Prato 46/7t, Fritz Prenzel 23br, Hans Reinhard 22r, 24cl, Leonard Lee Rue 15tr, Michael Viard 19crb, Rod Williams 24cla; **DLP Communications:** David Heald 38/9c; **Chris Fairclough Colour Library:** 16bl; **Foods From Spain:** 31bl; **Fullwood:** 17c; **Robert Harding:** 21tc, 38bl, 38tr, 41tc, 41cb, 46br, 47tr, Christopher Rennie 14bl; **Holt Studios International:** Richard Anthony 9bl, D. Donne Bryant 11tr, 11cr, Nigel Cattlin 10/11t, 13cra, 21cla, 18cl, 25tr, 34cl, 35c, 36br, 39cla, 42c, 43br, Jurgen Dielenschneider 15cb, Jane Memmott 28cb, Primrose Peacock 26cl, 37c, Gordon Roberts 22tl, Inga Spence 32/3clb; **The Hutchison Library:** Victor Lamont 9c, Lesley McIntyre 9tl; S.Satushek 3c; **The Image Bank:** Terje Rakke 5tl, 27t, S. Satushek 3c, Frank Wing 32c, Trevor Wood 27cl; **Images:** 1c, endpapers; **Nature Photographers Ltd.:** Paul Sterry 19cb; **Oxford Scientific Films:** G.I. Bernard 25tc, Michael Fogden 46tr, Hans Reinhard 21c, Frank Schneidermeyer 24clb; **Panos Pictures:** 27cr, Ron Giling 46bl; **Harry Smith:** 31cr, 36br, 37cl; **Still Pictures:** Mark Edwards 40cl; **Tony Stone Worldwide:** Barry Lewis 20/21c, Stefan Reiss 23tc; **Survival Anglia:** John & Irene Palmer 8c, Michael Pitts 47bc; **Malvin Van Gelderen:** Jane Miller Collection 25cr; **Max Whitaker:** 14cl; **Wildlife Matters:** 47tc; **Zefa:** 15cra, T.J.Zhejiang 42bl.

c – **center**	cb – **center below**	clb – **center left below**	r – **right**	crb – **center right below**
cr – **center right**	cl – **center left**	cr – **center right**	bl – **bottom left**	cra – **center right above**
t – **top**	tr – **top right**	tl – **top left**	tc – **top center**	br – **bottom right**

INDEX